THE GREEN GIRLS

THE GREEN GIRLS

John Blair

Lena-Miles Wever Todd Poetry Series
PLEIADES PRESS
Warrensburg, Missouri
& Rock Hill, South Carolina

ISBN 0-8071-2855-4

Published by Pleiades Press
Department of English & Philosophy
Central Missouri State University
Warrensburg, Missouri 64093
&
Department of English
Winthrop University
Rock Hill, SC 29733

Distributed by Louisiana State University Press

2 4 6 8 9 7 5 3 1
First Pleiades Press Printing, 2003

Original cover art © Sandra Hoekman-Blair

Grateful acknowledgement is due to the following publications in which some of these poems, or versions thereof, originally appeared:
Black Warrior Review: "Pig Days"
Cimarron Review: "The Swimmer's Dressing Room at the Y"
The Georgia Review: "Running Away" (as "Old Man Walking")
Hampden-Sydney Poetry Review: "Mercy"
Kansas Quarterly/Arkansas Review: "The Weather Child"
Lullwater Review: "Salvage" (as "The Singing House")
Midwest Poetry Review: "Crazy Jane Watches the Dancers"
New Orleans Review: "The Rigolets"
New York Quarterly: "The Green Girls" (as "The Groves")
Plains Poetry Journal: "Handling Serpents"
Poetry: "Cicada" and "Winter Storm, New Orleans"
The Sewanee Review: "Madness and Love" and "Breath"
Texas Review: "Weathering"

CONTENTS

Shall it be male or female? say the fingers
That chalk the walls with green girls and their men.
—*Dylan Thomas*

. . . Paradise
is a place that must be left behind.
—*Howard Moss*

I. SALVAGE

Cicada

A youngest brother turns seventeen with a click as good as a roar,
finds the door and is gone.
You listen for that small sound, hear a memory.
The air-raid sirens howled of summer tornadoes, the sound

thrown back against the scattered thumbs
of grain silos and the open Oklahoma plains
like the warning wail of insects.
Repudiation is fast like a whirlwind.

Only children don't know that all you live is leaving.
Yes, the first knowledge that counts is that everything stops.
Even in the bible-belt, second comings are promises
you never really believed;

so you turn and walk into the embrace of the world
as you would to a woman, an arrant
an orphic movement as shocking as the subtle
animal pulse of a flower opening, palm up.

We are all so helpless.
I can look at my wife's full form now
and hope for children,
picture her figured by the weight of babies.

Only, it's still so much like trying to find something
once lost. My brother felt the fullness of his years, the pull
in the gut that's almost sickness. His white
smooth face is gone into living and fierce illusion,

a journey dissolute and as immutable
as the whining heat of summer.
Soon enough, too soon, momentum just isn't enough.
Our tragedy is to live in a world

that doesn't invite us back.
We slow, find ourselves sitting in a room that shifts so slightly
we can only imagine the difference.
I want to tell him to listen.

I want to tell him what it is to crave darkness,
to want to crawl headfirst into a dirt-warm womb
to sleep, to wait seventeen years,
to emerge again.

SALVAGE

Nothing is content with what it is,
the days dropping away like crusts,
already stale as tears. White stucco

crawled over the skinned
and boned body of the church
my father bought for salvage,

for burned acid of old wiring,
for plaster figured with a pointillier
of fungus, for sun thrown back

bright as a fender from the walls,
all of it, in all of its aged
and mysterious parts, ours,

right down to the desiccated body
of Christ raining yellow
through the air, swollen with mold.

We dragged it away in pieces like the past,
and burned it, as it should be burned,
under the calm face of the moon

where it stumbled dumb
through weeds, through pine needles,
through the palest of lives,

blinded by the relentless
stars that go on and on
until even the most

terrible passion for all
the far and savaged world
is, finally, overcome.

DRAGGING FOR THE DEAD

Our fathers sink slowly, going
beyond us, beyond living in their powerless weight,
the black tobacco smell of them,

their faces growing emptier and older,
and deeper.
There's not much to do

after those who struggle toward miracles
have come and gone with treble hooks
big as baskets but wait,

watching for a form to break slowly
white through the surface like a lie,
unburying itself wondrously.

So we go. The evening is always clear,
doves huddling in their gray mourning on mile
after mile of swayed power line,

each black eye watching
the same thing, the same
run of water sinking breathlessly

into itself over and over again.
Whoever we are, we've come
a long way to get here, we're eager

to get it over with, to walk above
the river among the graves and find
whatever it is we've come to find,

something deep in the cells
like the spark that makes a muscle move, your hand
close itself into a fist and tremble

in a way you can't control.
We want what we want and it shines,
following us like smoke into the vacuum

a body creates wherever it goes,
even when it goes here,
where we wait for our fathers,

for safe passage, for quiet evenings,
our eyes closed against the light,
or for that moment when the doves

will all at once take flight for no reason at all,
or maybe for the next breath to follow the last,
just because it must, and because

it always has.

OLEANDER

In 1967, in Cartersville, Georgia
a drunk flew his car into the open arms
of the girl who lived next door to us,

his Buick blowing through her
like a squall. She was sixteen,
walking home with someone else's

six-year-old son. At the last
thin instant she heaved the kid
like a stone into a weedy ditch.

What I wonder now is how
he must have felt, that boy,
finding himself alone, cradled

in the stiff winter mud, remembering
that girl, so quick, who had pitched
him away forever.

Lao Tse wrote that eternity
is the return to destiny,
which is the salt and clay and sky, which is

the fluid arc of what has been, forever
becoming us: maybe I was that boy in the ditch,
maybe I lay there in the mist

with the gray light of morning cool
on my face and listened to the car engine
ticking like a locust

as it cooled, waiting for a reason to move,
smelling burned rubber and weeds,
antifreeze, roadside oleander

with its poisonous flowers broad
as magnolia blossoms. Maybe I could hear
the tiny sounds of insects fingering through the debris

like haruspices looking for reasons and so
I understood all at once what the world intended
with its oleander bitter as death

or the things unsaid or the hard
pavement of roads
running away from us endlessly,

how we stand up from the mud to wait for it,
arms flung wide, braced for whatever might be coming,
whatever's already here.

WINTER STORM, NEW ORLEANS

If it could, the earth would wash
you and all of us from her as a lover

washes away experience. Winter, even here,
is the shudder of flesh touched by foulness.

The mud pulls at your feet
like sorrow. If you try, you can even find

comfort in the dead smell of coat-leather;
for a moment the wind is the voice of grief,

slashes inward with a fistful of cold rain,
then dissolves too into insensible drizzle.

The idea of snow is wrong here.
So you watch for it,

the random lights dropping
new through the trees, Yankee

whiteness to change your life.
The wind stumbles across the street

and is gone. The city settles
like the weathered ruin it always was.

CHRIST OF ST. JOHN OF THE CROSS

Dali's *Christ of Saint John of the Cross*
sags helplessly face-down over blue water,
over the copper-and-death smell of deep water,

over stolid hills and boats, his back
to God who has forsaken him. He has closed
his eyes to Eden, to the whole of the world

steamed open beneath him like a letter,
the evening drying like a moth out of its wrinkles,
as spare as a saint's cell, a breath,

a flutter, a little trembling green—paradise, wet
and pierced through with love or prelapsarian joy
or some incredible arcing light

of redemption that crackles,
almost makes it, and then fails endlessly,
sinking toward a rocky bottom like the gelded

passions of angels. Whatever glory there was
already bled away, sunwashed like old paint
or like the promise of redemption, broken

and muddy with tears. Renunciation,
shadows on walls, odd shapes in the clouds,
small pleasures, fish cooked by the sea,

the comfortable grind of metal on wood
as a plane peels away coppery leaves
from a plank of cedar.

All the occasions of paradise that gather
like benedictions beneath the broad
and startled face of God. Like us,

he will long for them in the dirt and ashes
of forever. Like us, he only wishes
he was coming back to stay.

BREATH

Winter, and the gulf
draws in like a consumptive, ochre
dead sea milking the marshes for breath—

Nothing else shows the least ambition, lingering
naked behind the thin scrim of oil-glare
like a kiss of fluorescence on the line of the horizon.

A bridge pulses, headlights white and wired tight
over a tug groaning against its leash,
phosphor burning in its catholic wake,

flushed gratefully out of the river's mouth,
past the shudder of channel lights
into the salt-stung body of the sea.

The ice on the river is almost
thick enough to walk on,
a settled mist dissolving

across the water where
the trees open out into a field.
Here, in the brittleness of the weeds,

where a bull sidles up to rub
his broad hip against a post, his lopsided
testicles swinging in their red-haired sac

pendulous in the fog
as a drop of blood poised over porcelain,
you can kneel on graves so old

there aren't any stones and you can wait,
in the honeysuckle and the briars,
while the mist of the whole world's

spoken breath rises from the ground,
swept to a place where nothing,
not even words, can redeem it.

II. Mercy

MERCY

Over her head under the porch eaves
a mud-dauber throbs
in a brown tube of numbed spiders,
single-minded and alone.

She's afraid of the wasps,
but not so much that she can make herself
break up the rows of tubes
so that the pale yellow larvae

fall to the porch floor
and wriggle out their half-formed lives.
When she was thirteen she saw her mother
follow a Persian cat out behind the greenhouse winking

with sun and she saw how the cat hid
under an Azalea bush full of red blossoms
like stigmata. She watched as her mother waited,
and when the cat had dropped its litter

how her mother took each kitten
and broke its soft neck, her fingers
kneading the sticky fur
like red Georgia clay,

as if she were making small figures
of her simple mercy.
Her life feels loose in her hands like seeds;
she swims in the lake every day,

even in the winter when she has to walk
into a coldness that laps
around the pilings of the boathouse,
like skin on skin above the mud and silt.

She once came so close to drowning there, her arms
and legs growing heavy and brilliant,
and what saved her was a raft made of steel drums
and two-by-fours anchored like a wooden moon

on the water's blessed horizon.
Careless excesses of effort, and pain
that grows like fatigue in the fingers,
the raw meshing of bones in the knees,

strain spreading iridescent as oil.
And still, every evening the struggle
to rise beyond the first surge up
from the bottom's heavy mud

into gliding swiftly under pale stars
like sparks burning out from under
the sliding bulk of the world,
dust scrubbed loose

and raining through the planet's raw light,
into the thin air she breathes in
on every third stroke. The water
makes her bones feel bird-delicate

and weightless, so that she thinks about
her own bitter womb, and her mother
holding a cat, its head cradled like a baby's
in the warm, empty cup of her hand.

Running Away

She's heading south, to paradise, to palm trees
on streets lined with stucco and green deep grass.
Near midnight she's stopped on a shoulder near Ocalla,
the car faithless, cattle everywhere, indifferent as God.

Just breathe, she says, and bodies everywhere do.
She remembers sumacs blushing
damp with all their new buds
and a shed blunt with the smell of grease

where dust flowered and burned to glittering ash
on hubcaps pinned by the palms to the walls.
She was twelve or thirteen. Everything
was there, the whole of her life

in the droning heat where she was moth-dirt
and little girl, abandoned in the half-light
casket-closeness of herself,
nothing moving except the liquid patterns

of mirages on dust a mile away,
the sour drifting yellow of smoke
from stump fires, the stuttering
of telephone poles along a road

that was only a hint at endlessness, a breath
bright-edged with salt, a sea yearning
towards dryness, the horizon swamp-hammocked
and shimmering in the heat.

There's too much of anyplace. Starlight clings
like dust on the one bulb that burns
the whole moon like a doll's glass eye,
a word tethered at the end

of the road, the night barbed
and strung with stars sharp
as hooks. All around hunkers
the buckshot depths of swamp,

the septic, bare smell of disappointment.
The road like an annunciation runs
above batture and river bloom.
On a grassy shoulder she watches

a city's lights flicker far away over lovers arced
and mingling like fireflies, winking
like they know her. She sits, rat's nest,
broken-motor in her dreams, and listens to a river

humming to her its loneliness,
how it aches with rocks and hidden roots,
how it knows that nothing compels us but ourselves,
just the blunt currents of our hearts,

and maybe the moon swimming
through the sifting fingers of the willows,
its dead doll's eye on heaven,
its cowed yellow back showing us the way.

THE LESSER BODIES OF THE SOLAR SYSTEM

1.

A few of the lesser bodies of the solar system
pass us close, the asteroids Adonis, Apollo,
Geographos and Hermes. Lonely falling Icarus.

And Eros, the largest of the close-approach asteroids,
potato-shaped and ugly, glancing away
fourteen million miles short of killing us all.

The clock-ticking of the wind brushing
though the palmettos outside the window
is as plain as penance, as patent as new leaves

stirring their pale undersides like hands,
tender with the cool blood of roots.

2.

She is Sunday morning reading, churchworn,
a page of loveliness, creased and faithless.

She stirs and the mattress moans with what it knows.
She grows supple under the bright wings of her longing.
What she's thinking is an exchange: all I have for all I want.

It always ends like this, a cursory spill of clouds
in the windows, daylight pooling in the calm
blue corners, one more testimony to the stammer
of momentum becoming nothing at all.

Her face is watermarked like linen, like the sky swept clean
except for a few weary mare's tales. There's no place
somewhere else enough, inertia like a wire tied
around the salt pillar of her spine.

3.

The bells tremolo a catholic question and she opens
and stretches her doubt. She wants to believe only
in the clean mercies of physics, in the arcs
and eccentricities of bodies in their orbits.

Should Eros ever show its oblong
and descending shape in our sky, the cities
will rage with desperate seductions.
Everyone knows this, everyone secretly hopes for it.

Some one hundred tons of meteoric material
strikes the earth every long day of our lives,
a few small meteorites, usually,
and 99 tons of fine sifting dust like flakes of skin.

It's why the bells are ringing, the lesser bodies
calling us with their devout and linear contritions
into our own blind trajectories,
our own peculiar impacts.

At one hundred tons a day, it will take four million years
for the surface of the world to be buried beneath
a single blowzy millimeter, a fact too disappointing
to think about.

Outside the windows, gulls
scree and cough until the glass rattles
with their unhappiness.

4.

She remembers her Emerson: *Every man
is an infinitely repelling orb.*

There comes a point when whatever you hear
sounds like the word *please*
said over and over again until it glosses
every surface like a film.

The week always ends like this, the universe
bending to her its subtle gravities, every grainy day
coming back on itself in perfect faith.

She's already missing it. One look back
and she can already see
the fine arc of her return.

WEATHERING

She shredded the flowers
he brought her because she found them

insincere, left them where he could find them,
swept like raw snow, flakes of blood,

across the table, in the sink.
Last year, early in September, they'd driven

to a beach-house in the keys, where the sun was
bright enough to burn away lies, spent

the short weekend wading, throwing spoiled shrimp
to the gulls, trying to lose the tension

in the moody rustling of the surf.
The last afternoon they scraped the rain-soaked ash

from a pit on the beach. They replaced the ash
with pine boards he found under the house.

He stuffed newspaper underneath
and they waited for the night to move down.

When the fire was burning they watched
the lights on the wet gray sand,

felt the slow, sepulchral sweeping of the waves
moving in and out. They sat for as long

as the boards lasted. In the darkness
he touched her and she felt how something inside

had grown dry, spreading across their faces
in a quick tightening of sunburned skin.

Home again, she thinks about how the mist puffing
through the curtains smells like the sea,

and so does her husband where he sleeps. It's the same,
the salty weathered smell, some things dead,

others carrying on as they always have.
Nothing left really but mornings when the light

will wake her, streaks filled with dust, tiny lost fragments
of them both, gathering in the corners like snow.

Only, she knows how easy it is
to wonder whether she will outlive him,

whether he will go before her suddenly,
without pain, into that one thing they will certainly share.

She will grieve, of course. There will be the stolid
gray breast of family, stony fish waiting in the waves,

rain that blooms from the sand like memory letting go,
the long days still to come

settling out between them, somehow emptier,
bright and still, like torn flowers.

At Seventy, Visited by Her Son

Stranger, she'll say, give me your hand, be the odd goblin
I always knew you were, popping up out of absence

where there's no one who's stranger,
no one who's you.

Don't be afraid. This is a body
you should take the time to know

like you've never known your own, a body
that's only body. Flesh that's only flesh, holy

or not, clean or not, mine or not, pretty much
all the same, just *body*.

You understand *hungry*, of course, or you think you do,
the way the eyes narrow and the tongue comes out, stiff

piece of meat, ineloquent. The perennial flower
of appetite is grown seasonal, comes

when it comes but always, so far, comes,
and watching it turn, you are my one apostle.

O, bud and leaf and brown limbs akimbo! O, little cloister
in the trees, holy with waiting!

Grow small, I tell myself, shrivel, grow tears like leaves—
after all, there's nowhere else you'll be going but here.

Flesh is a blessing, and like all blessings,
wears on us until we stop.

I want you to tell me something: I want you to cry out
hold me, hold me tight! Pass on the gray wampum

of your heart's love! Listen to the slap slap
of a nurse's holy white shoes, bringing salvation! Listen!

I will say to you, listen, the heart never stops
though it withers and lies forever

a black fist where all your life used to be.

SHE DREAMS OF A BOY DROWNING

In her dream, he's floating under the branches
of an orange tree where it leans over a pond,
roots torn out, green oranges hard as lies,
crisp with acid.

She's watching him, drifting in the green water.
He's the one she's always wanted
for as long as she's wanted,
skin slick as moss, hair spread

like a huge hand laid palm down on the back of his head.
She can feel the water tight
around his temples rippling like a trachea.
Her hands curl like leaves

Around his breathlessness, a great cetacean moan
out of the darkness where the world begins.
What it means is the calm root and wheel of her surrender.
What it means is that she will never live enough.

III. The Green Girls

In the Swimmer's Dressing Room at the Y

Saturday morning, the dressing room
empty, smelling of chlorine. If I listen,

I can hear my wife on the other side
in a space that holds back everything

but the small bright sounds spilling
through the vent at the top of the one

common wall. If I listen, watching
the place before the door where daylight

rages in its narrow square over
a single round drain dimpled in

like a fish's eye, if I listen, ready
and pale and sitting on a wooden bench soft

with the smell of water and sweat,
I can salvage the familiar, wife-simple, in little steps.

Acolyte, hands ready on my knees,
I wonder if other women watch her,

if she watches herself in the mirrors
at the end of every row of lockers, pale

buttocks and stomach white against
the gray and blue, steel and tile.

On this side, old men pass through
from the brightness of the entrance

to the brightness of the exit, thin shanked
and intent, not so blinded they can't see.

So I listen for my wife, for the softest
rustlings of cloth swept across skin, rising

through hair, the horsefly-drone of a bulb burning
above pooled water, bare bodies like a hum

over the wet woman shower smell. And when I hear
a slap that could be a foot on tile, or buttocks

on the wet salty boards of the benches,
I walk completely, barefoot-careful

into the sunny space before the pool,
blinded by light thrown up from the water

where someone bathing shades her eyes
to watch us while we stand there, almost touching

in the clarity our white bodies make, flush
with clean sunlight and bright, bright water.

The Southern Lights

Jackson's dead now because driving
road equipment for thirty years in the hot Florida sun
turned him black and breathlessly cancerous.
We all know he beat my aunt until she left him,
and I remember how, having nothing,
he'd take my cousins out on his weekends
in his yellow Buick Wildcat
and let them drive,

eight or nine years old, on some thin dirt road
cut through the palmetto and slash pine
out in the county where no one cares, trying
to buy them back, until the sorrow gathered
so he was dusky with it
and crying and ashamed
and now dead, and I shouldn't care,
but my God I do,

and I know how the living grease of our years
renders itself out through our skins like sweat
until we are all the same dark prospects of regret
abiding in the wilderness. Across the lake,
ripples shake in drifts along the green backs
of snakes stolid in their laziness
and Orion drops over the horizon's
thin blue lip, liquid

above the geography of our penitence.
Boats rock in the echo of a faraway wake
like a lesson: it all comes back.
What touches us here
is all we can know to want
and so we sit, locked in forgiveness
as ruthless as the cold waters
of our love. I'll tell you and you only,

we are bright angels, and God in his garden
lives alone in a perfection we will never know
in this southern, forever fallen place. Kiss me,
one sharp blow to the forehead swift as a hammer,
spend this sleepless night with me, apart from every evil.
The world, as it does, will roll on without us, and where
it will end up is even stranger than this darkness
we have, at least, grown used to.

MADNESS AND LOVE

. . . for the purposes of tragedy, the two passions of madness and love . . .
—Longinus, *On the Sublime*

The first time we are boys: the woman is bright
and glossed, alive in the rippling of paper, tense

between children who want so badly a white
body turned the red of brass in the dense

light of someone's cellar where, as if he could
make it more tolerable, *Jesus*

falls like a drop from every boy's tongue,
all of us feeling the first bone-touch

of the one meaning of love a twelve-year-old
can know, drained pale by the shock of so much

so suddenly letting go. And then
it is you, and everything you love

is a woman or the meaning of one,
passion so great we gather it to us

like the morning gathering light, the sun
migrating to the blur of sheets, the bulk

of our lives spent waiting
for the thin, rare streaks of this kind of joy,

the prismatic shimmer of hair, the gut-tightening
like a knife-stroke.

THE WEATHER CHILD

Wind is the suffering of spirit. . . .
—Fred Chappell

Wind blows dust from the road high in the air like a thunderhead, rising
under buzzards piled in the broad gyre of their watchfulness.
I can feel under my wife's skin something beating like starlight
on the back of the eye,

just that steady, a murmur that promises *everything,*
everything, everything. Outside, the pass and sough of wind

in the cedars sounds like the first low rush of a heart heard through
the distance of flesh, lisping like a ghost in the Doppler.

Last winter our first child ended with the season, in the last cold rains
of March. This daughter or son feels the same tidal pull, tugs
and bleeds at our fear. The day darkens toward sleet, drizzling
down in careless streaks. The wind swells into a restless flagellation,

every leaf a scourge beating back grief, every sound full
of the cupped-wing terror of birds caught in a sky

that spoils under clouds tender and black as frostbitten skin.
But we've learned. Now we are willing to settle for breaking even,
for the frank and steady odds of the world's indifference.
We know tomorrow will come, pale and drawn like new skin.

The wind will settle. A new day will drop clean as baptism
into the blue hollows of our sleeplessness. The air will clear.

Birds will ease back into the trees where the light nests in splinters,
their small bones clattering like lullabies in the careless breeze.

PIG DAYS

September was for the butcher's knife, for hogs
hung by the heels, blood strung like saliva, turning black.

Rain came, puddling new life into old blood,
slipping red up wet grass like veins, viscera reaching to a head

wrapped in burlap and left for the flies. Pastures steamed.
We yearned for the cool end of summer, for evenings blue

with the last throb of light on the coy and clinging leaves
and for you, the dead, humble as a shadow, rising

into the clear lake of our lives, the sky bitter with rain and with
the yellow straw of your small ghost's coming back to us;

much as we might try, nothing ever stays the way we leave it.
The rain brings it back again, livid as Indian summer.

Pinned under the broad grind of the turning stars
the good pain begins. Frost gathers in the brittle evening air.

One deep breath and it settles, crisp as grief, onto the blood-black grass.

CRAZY JANE WATCHES THE DANCERS

Love is all/ Unsatisfied/ That cannot take the whole/ Body and soul.
— W. B. Yeats

There they are,
stuck to each other like flies.

When we were young John
pitched me out a window once, straight

through the glass. Not a scratch, but
I bode my time, took up a lamp, mighty

sword of retribution, and smote him where he lay,
drunken-idle and snoring. Jesus! Did he roar!

Half of love is pain, and half of that is giving it: look, you'd
almost think there's music, the way the bodies sway.

They waltz their passions through the trees, and sometimes
into the bushes where the light don't go, just patch

of skin here, patch of skin there through the leaves
like a painting: Still Life with Fleshtones.

Still, god bless 'em for their optimism. I know.
I've seen where it all goes, that skin slick as butter,

those supple lovely bones: into bruises and damnation
and the bawl and stroke of corruption.

Take it while you can, honey. Love isn't a lion's tooth
but a hen's, and damned scarce.

The Green Girls

Local girls, born brown-skinned and lake-eyed,
knowing the difference and still as inevitably

as the first rusting of menses, suddenly,
without even understanding why, flat on their backs

in a place where everything is green.
It's summer. The day is worn, sunlight working its way

through leaves detailing the tilled earth, leaf mold,
blossoms swollen soft over the promise of fruit;

the sand bears the imprints of battered Fords, spots of oil
spilt like the careless passion of backseats.

A radio wavers at the edge of hearing, tuned
to the ether, a susurrus that almost cries "daughters!"

before fading into the sound of breath, the crackle of sweat.
From the heart of the grove a dry

breeze flows slick as powdered skin,
bringing with it whispers soaked

with the rooted strumming of trees, as light
and as muted as bare green bodies breathing in.

Rain Dancing

It's love again, my friend,
the sky impenetrable and trailing,

the two of us bellied in the rain and naked
in a field of soybeans, mud-fat, dead-air, hands

sizzling like the cars nearby on the highway,
the wind stroking fingers across our backs

licking at our faces like a rust-colored dog
just wild to be gone.

Hold me, hold me, rigid as rain,
cold sluice of compulsion, vines akimbo,

dirteaters, sandlappers, mud-humped,
red-skinned, making beasts in the field,

hasped in our coupling, and locked
in the fertile clay we're made of.

IV. The Orders of Absence

THE LOST BOYS

Their voices rustle like the amber burr
of wasps. They smell of pollen and the green breath
of goats. They hide in the yellow grass or stand
waist-deep in the rank water of a cattle pond,

their voices shrill and impossible
under the huge and spinning firmament.
Something clanks in the wind like
a tin school bell against the rusted body

of a tractor that died in its row—
they are the small voices of all
the lost children, God's angels, watching you,
eyes glittering with the stunned green

of bottleflies. You hear them in the trees
when the wind blows and the upper branches
become haunted with wanderlust,
throwing twigs and leaves like orphans.

They can smell the budging stink
of your aging soul as well as you can.
Thin voices hum inside your ear like mosquitoes,
saying *never, never, never*

until the night disappears into the withered body of day
like a breath drawn carefully, in secret.

THE ORDERS OF ABSENCE

In Louisiana is a leper colony,
the only one in North America,
kept by the Daughters of Charity
for the afflicted though there aren't many

anymore and the Haitian man
named Michael who walks us
through the wards and the chapel
seems contrite and lonely

in his duties, shaking our hands
as we leave, his own hand
as fingerless and round as a fisher's loaf.
No worries, not contagious

really, you have to live with a leper
to become a leper, though we wonder
who can risk the compelling exposures
of affection? No one,

we're sure. Outside the summer heat
makes the azaleas' leaves
hang limp and rude as dog's tongues.
All of this was plantation,

Michael tells us, and he's proud of that,
and the neatness of the grounds,
the clean cicatrices on the trunks
of the live-oaks where they've been trimmed.

The hospital was the big house, of course,
and keeps its cool air of propriety, nuns
in winged habits gathered humble
under the tall ceilings

to minister and to wait.
This is what we do, they seem to say, though
they say nothing at all, at least to us:
we accept what is gone,

what's dissolved, what's never coming back.
The world is cruel.
Of course it is, we want to tell them.
What else could keep us

to our complacencies, the safety
of our private griefs, our
privileged losses? An order of absence
laves our every moment

with suffering. But we've come here, after all,
a kind of communion
with the sorrows of the flesh,
with the mercies of care,

with the borrowed bones of us all.
Look at us, oddly happy.
Stooping in the breathless heat
to smell the flowers in a leper's garden,

smiling like a picture someone should take
and waving to everyone our five-fingered good-byes.

THE RIGOLETS

Hours ago and ten miles south he had run, weeping,
into the Saint Louis Cathedral shouting *I am Jesus Christ*

and murdered angels with a two foot
piece of iron rebar, marble wings

cracking like ice, a stiff beseeching finger
skidding under a pew. Now he's here, where

the water lies under a scrim of oil-glare,
throwing the sunset back so blinding

it could be some kind of miracle he might
kneel before, his knees hard on the bright

scree of pounded angel or deep in the binding
and amniotic mud, the pale pane of his forehead

flat on water gray as marrow, cupped in the font
of the world. The channel spreads by degrees

under the tide. He's shaking in every
part and he's crying hard, mostly because

it's done and over with and ten miles away
and still nothing is what anyone would want,

just these back inlets silted with worn-out tires,
muddy as old God, corrugated like oystershells,

lousy with trout fry and water skaters,
its warm breath on his shoulder

smelling of the kind of dreams
that can't be helped.

O, Jesus, he says, because it's still there like a cramp
in his chest, ambition risen with the moon's blue

list, so cold there was nothing to do but to take
steel in hand and go, gripped with conviction,

into the calm sanctuary, drunken
with a fact incredible as crucifixion,

swinging, shouting out what has to be true,
I am the one, the holy, redeemer, come back for you.

HANDLING SERPENTS

Easter, and somewhere under the sandy hiss
of the rain a snake's mouth opens

vulva-pink behind the worm-flicker of a tongue
lifting sweat off a forearm in some backwoods church,

worm-sick crackers sweating joy.
No confessions there, no persuasions,

no Come As Thou Art, just a little tremor
at the root of the tongue where revelation lives

and God thick as a horse's dick in the palm
of your hand, swaying in His jaws with deliverance.

There's a spring storm full of bluster
going outside, rain stuttering through its sermon,

and you think that that is how He will save you,
if He can save you, in godawful, god-blessed

ignorance, drawing the sin out like a poison
through the knotty chambers of your heart

where faith cramps in the muscle like that tooth
you saved for luck, the pure spirit shuddering

in the sanctuary of the bowels like a promise you can pass on
in the coiled and sure stroke of grace: lidless eyes

to stare you clean again, a kiss to pull you into paradise,
curled in the poisoned grief of His love, never knowing

until it is no longer yours whether God will take you
or leave you.

COMFORT

The season's just a little apologetic,
shrugging off its tremens, its bleary-eyed
hopefulness. We won't believe

in resurrections less qualified
than this, protestant and as gray
as bark, dissolute

with its burden of rain.
Even mourners are all so long gone
the only reason to come would be to say a prayer

for mercy where a little rain has pooled
like amber in the soaked layers
of leaves, lost in the leaf-mold

with the billion dead swaddled
underfoot like larvae. On every corner
their chaste mouths have gnawed

the edges bright as the sky huge
with its last promise to love them
back to life, one bloom

of a door to let them spill back in, green
noose of starting over like
a whole new world of troubles.

About the Author

John Blair's *The Green Girls* was selected by Cornelius Eady for the Lena-Miles Wever Todd Poetry Series. Blair's poems appear in *Poetry, Georgia Review, New Letters,* and elsewhere and his short story collection, *American Standard,* won the 2002 Drue Heinz Award. He lives in Texas with his wife and son.

About the Lena-Miles Wever Todd Poetry Series

The editors and directors of the Lena-Miles Wever Todd Poetry Series select one book of poems for publication by Pleiades Press and Winthrop University each year. All selections are made blind to authorship in an open competition for which any American poet is eligible. Past winners include Matthew Cooperman for *A Sacrificial Zinc* (Susan Ludvigson, final judge), Al Maginnes for *The Light in Our Houses* (Betty Adcock, final judge) and Kevin Prufer for *Strange Wood* (Andrea Hollander Budy, final judge).